Okapis

By Christy Steele

Steadwell
Books

Raintree
A Division of Reed Elsevier, Inc.

Chicago, Illinois

www.raintreelibrary.com

ANIMALS OF THE RAIN FOREST

For information, address the publisher:
Raintree, 100 N. LaSalle, Suite 1200, Chicago, IL 60602

Library of Congress Cataloging-in-Publication Data
Steele, Christy.
  Okapis / Christy Steele.
      v. cm. -- (Animals of the rain forest)
Includes bibliographical references (p.   ).
Contents: Range map for okapis -- Okapis in the rain forest -- What okapis eat -- An okapi's life cycle -- The future of okapis.
  ISBN 0-7398-6839-X (lib. bdg.-hardcover)
  1. Okapi--Juvenile literature. [1. Okapi.] I. Title. II. Series.
  QL737.U56 S74 2003
  599.638--dc21
                              2002015211
Printed and bound in the United States of America

Produced by Compass Books

Photo Acknowledgments
Wildlife Conservation Society/D. Demello, cover, 1, 6, 8, 10, 12, 14, 21, 24; Root Resources/Kenneth W. Fink, 16, 22, 28-29; Visuals Unlimited/Ken Lucas, 18; Chuck Dressner, 26.

Content Consultants
Dr. Cynthia Bennett
Research Curator
Dallas Zoo, Texas

Joan Daniels Tantillo
Assistant Curator, Mammal Department
Chicago Zoological Society, Brookfield Zoo
Brookfield, Illinois

This book supports the National Science Standards.

Some words are shown in bold, **like this**. You can find out what they mean by looking in the Glossary.

Contents

Range Map of Okapis

MOROCCO
TUNISIA
Canary Islands (SPAIN)
ALGERIA
LIBYA
EGYPT
WESTERN SAHARA
MAURITANIA
MALI
NIGER
SENEGAL
GAMBIA
GUINEA BISSAU
BURKINA
CHAD
Lake Chad
SUDAN
DJIBOUTI
GUINEA
BENIN
SOMALIA
SIERRA LEONE
IVORY COAST
TOGO
GHANA
NIGERIA
ETHIOPIA
Lake Turkana
LIBERIA
CAMEROON
CENTRAL AFRICAN REPUBLIC
EQUATORIAL GUINEA
Lake Albert
UGANDA
South Atlantic
GABON
CONGO
KENYA
Lake Victoria
RWANDA
DEMOCRATIC REPUBLIC OF THE CONGO
BURUNDI
TANZANIA
Lake Tanganyika
MALAWI
Lake Nyasa
ANGOLA
ZAMBIA
Lake Kariba
MOZAMBIQUE
NAMIBIA
ZIMBABWE
MADAGASCAR
BOTSWANA
SWAZILAND
LESOTHO
SOUTH AFRICA

N
W E
S

Range of Okapis
Surrounding Land
Water
Borders
Rivers

A Quick Look at Okapis

What do okapis look like?

Okapis have a long neck topped with a thin head. Their bodies are like a horse's with long legs and hooves. They have unusual markings. Their dark-brown bodies are marked with white or gray patches around the face and neck. White zebra-like stripes are on their backside and upper legs. The very bottoms of their back legs are white. Male okapis have two fur-covered horns.

Where do okapis live?

Okapis live only in the Ituri Forest, which is in the Democratic Republic of the Congo in Africa.

What do okapis eat?

Okapis eat only plants. They eat up to 100 different kinds of plants, including grasses, leaves and fruit.

Okapis are sometimes called forest giraffes.

Okapis in the Rain Forest

Okapis are some of the hardest animals to find and study in the wild. They live deep in Africa's Ituri rain forest and usually hide when people come near.

Okapis belong to the Giraffidae family. The only other member of this family is the giraffe. However, okapis have shorter necks and different markings than giraffes do. But both giraffes and okapis have sloping backs, extra-long tongues, and the males have furry horns.

The scientific name for okapis is *Okapia johnstoni*. *Johnstoni* comes from the name Harry Johnston. In 1901 Johnston became the first European to see an okapi. *Okapia* comes from the animal's African name, *o'api*.

▲ This okapi is looking for food inside its home range.

Where do okapis live?

Wild okapis live only in Africa. There they make their homes in the Ituri Forest. This is a rain forest where many trees grow close together and a lot of rain falls. It has a rainy and a dry season. January is the driest month, while April and November are the wettest.

The Ituri Forest is a tropical rain forest in the Democratic Republic of the Congo (once named Zaire). Okapis spend most of their time in the northeastern part of the country, where the rain forest is the thickest.

Mountains cover part of the Ituri Forest. Okapis generally stay between 1,500 to 3,300 feet (500 to 1,000 meters) above sea level. Sea level is the average height of ocean water. Sometimes okapis might wander even higher to look for food. The highest sighting of an okapi was at 4,757 feet (1,450 meters) on Mount Hoyo. At this height, the days are hot and wet. The nights are cooler.

Each okapi has a home range. It lives and looks for food in this space. The size of the home range most likely depends on how many okapis are in one place and how much food is available. Males have larger home ranges of up to 4 square miles (10 square kilometers), while females live in smaller areas.

Several okapis may share parts of each other's home ranges. A male's home range will often overlap that of several different females. This is not a problem. Okapis prefer to live alone, but will usually not fight other okapis that come near.

▲ You can see this male okapi's fur-covered horn.

How are okapis and giraffes alike?

An okapi is an odd-looking animal. At first, people did not know what kind of animal it was. They thought it was a kind of zebra. Even though an okapi looks like a zebra, it has more in common with a gifaffe.

Like a giraffe, an okapi's head is long and thin. It has large eyes and strong, thin lips.

Mother okapis will fight to protect their young. They beat the ground with their hooves before they fight. Scientists believe okapis do this to scare away predators without fighting.

An okapi can move its big, rounded ears in different directions. Males have two short, knobby horns in front of their ears. Only giraffes and okapis have these special furry, skin-covered horns. Female okapis do not grow horns.

Both giraffes and okapis have long **prehensile** tongues. Prehensile means able to grip and grab. An okapi's bluish-black tongue can be a little more than 1 foot (.3 meters) long!

You can spot an okapi or giraffe's tracks because they have **cloven** hooves. Cloven means split. Okapis have two toes on each hoof, so each hoof looks like it is split in two.

Giraffids also walk differently than other animals. Their front legs are longer than their back legs. When they walk, they move both the front and back legs of one side at the same time. Many other animals move the legs of different sides instead.

An okapi's coloring helps camouflage it among the rain forest plants.

What do okapis look like?

Okapis are smaller than giraffes. They are only 5 to 6 feet (1.5 to 1.7 meters) tall at the shoulder and weigh from 450 to 700 pounds (205 to 317 kilograms). Females are often slightly larger than males.

Okapis have a long, thin tail with a patch of bushy hair on its end. By quickly moving the tail back and forth, an okapi can keep insects away.

Okapis have short, thick, soft fur and special markings. Their body is dark reddish-brown with gray or white cheeks. All okapis have white zebra-like stripes on their backsides and legs. Each okapi has its own pattern of stripes on its backside. The very bottoms of their back legs are white like socks.

Their striped leg and backside markings most likely provide **camouflage**. Camouflage is coloring or patterns that help an animal blend in with its natural surroundings. The brown fur helps an okapi blend in with the dark trees and plant growth of the rain forest floor. Sunlight streams through the leaves and creates shadows on the rain forest floor. An okapi's uneven stripes help break up the outline of its body. Because of this, its shape does not stand out in the shadows.

These okapis are eating leaves from rain forest trees.

What Okapis Eat

Okapis are **herbivores**. Herbivores eat only plants. Okapis eat mostly leaves from different plants, but they also eat some grasses. Fruits and ferns are some plants that okapis eat.

Scientists study okapi droppings to find out what they eat. They found out that okapis eat more than 200 different kinds of plants, but only 30 make up most of their diet. Usually okapis have no problem finding food because they eat so many kinds of things.

Okapis have special ways of getting the salt and other minerals their bodies need to stay healthy. One way is to eat clay from riverbanks. This clay has minerals in it. The minerals are absorbed (soaked up) as the clay passes through the okapi's body.

▲ This okapi is using its tongue to strip
leaves from the bush.

Finding food and eating

When okapis are hungry, they walk along trails
to find food. Okapis are browsers. Browsers eat
mostly buds and new leaves from trees.
Sometimes okapis graze, too. Grazers eat grasses
and plants that grow close to the ground.

An okapi's body has adapted to browsing. To
adapt means to change over time to be able to

survive in an environment. The okapis long neck helps it reach tree leaves. By stretching its long neck and using its long tounge, it can reach up to 8 feet (2.4 meters) high. To pick leaves, the okapi wraps its **prehensile** tounge around a branch. It strips the leaves from the branch as it pulls them into its mouth.

Okapis are **ruminants**. A ruminant has a stomach made up of different sections, or chambers. The okapi's stomach has four chambers. To eat, the okapi first briefly chews and swallows its food. The first part of the stomach begins breaking it down. Then, the okapi **regurgitates** the food. To regurgitate is to bring the food back up out of the stomach into the mouth. This food is like a soft mushy mass. The okapi chews it, usually 40 to 50 times, and swallows it again. The food then passes through the other three chambers of the stomach.

Special bacteria live in okapis' stomachs. Bacteria are small living things that live on, in, or around plants and animals. Okapis' stomach bacteria help them break down plants. Because of the bacteria and their special stomachs, okapis can eat plants that are poisonous to people.

This male is stretching his neck to put on a show for a female.

An Okapi's Life Cycle

Okapis are shy and are hard to find in the wild. Much of what we know about their behavior comes from studying okapis in zoos.

Okapis like to live alone. At times, several may be in the same area to eat. However, they usually only come together to mate.

Okapis begin mating when they are two to four years old. They can mate anytime during the year, but mating usually happens in May and June, or in November and December.

To find mates, males and females release special scents. They follow the scents until they find each other. Females may also call to the males.

Once they have found each other, the male raises and lowers one of his front legs. He taps the female with his leg. Then, they mate.

Young okapis

After mating, the male and female leave each other. The female goes into the thickest part of the forest. She finds a hidden place to give birth. After about 15 months, the female gives birth to one calf, usually during the rainy season.

The okapi calf can weigh up to 80 pounds (36 kilograms) at birth and can stand within 30 minutes. It begins **nursing**, or drinking its mother's milk, soon after birth.

After it is born, an okapi calf will choose a nest site. It often takes up to 3 days to pick a place. The calf hides in this nest for the next 2 months. It may spend up to 80 percent of its time resting there.

For most of the day, the mother leaves her calf. She eats and comes back only so her calf can nurse. After two months, the calf leaves the nest. It follows its mother around her home range.

After about six months, the okapi calf stops nursing. It then eats only plants. It learns which leaves to eat from its mother. She will often bend down and share the food in her mouth with her calf.

This mother okapi is protecting her young calf as they move around their home range.

After about nine months, the calf leaves its mother. A calf often stays in its mother's home range, but moves around without her. Sometimes a mother and her calf rejoin each other and travel together for a while.

Okapis in zoos can live for 30 years but usually live for 12 to 15 years. Scientists do not know how long wild okapis live.

This okapi is using its long tongue to clean its eyes and face.

An okapi's day

Okapis are **diurnal,** or active during the day. This helps them keep safe from **predators**. Leopards are their only natural predators, and these big cats usually sleep during the day.

Okapis spend most of their day eating. They will walk up to 2.5 miles (4 kilometers) each day to look for food.

They mark their home range as they walk around it. To do this, they rub their heads against trees. They also have special scent glands between their hooves. Glands are body parts that produce and release things the body needs. Okapis rub their scent around their home range with these glands. Males may also spray their home range with urine. This way, other okapis know the home range is taken or that some other okapi has been there.

A small part of an okapi's day is also spent **grooming,** or cleaning itself. They use their tongue to clean their fur. Because their tongue is so long, they even use it to clean their eyes, eyelids, and nostrils!

Okapi can communicate, or send messages, to each other. They make a "chuff" sound when they see other okapis. If an okapi is in danger or scared, it may bleat. This cry often comes from an okapi calf that has lost its mother.

Okapis usually do not fight. They have different ways of showing who is dominant. Dominant means powerful or stronger. Dominant males will kick, stretch their necks, and toss their heads. A weaker okapi might kneel and then lay down with its head and neck on the ground.

Okapis are some of the rarest animals in the world.

The Future of Okapis

Okapis are not listed as **endangered**. Endangered means that a species is in danger of dying out. Most scientists believe there is still a healthy number of okapis in the wild.

In 1932, laws were passed to protect okapis. It is against the law for people in the Democratic Republic of Congo to hunt them.

Today, political unrest and wars put the okapis in danger. Wars have forced more people to move into the forest where okapis live. This unrest also makes it dangerous for scientists to get into the area and see how okapis are doing.

Okapis' habits help keep them safe. A habit is a usual way of acting. They live in parts of the rain forest that are hard for people to reach. Okapis will also run and hide if they see people. This makes it hard for hunters to find or catch okapis.

▲ Okapis like to play with each other. They lower their heads, wag their tails, and run.

What will happen to okapis?

Okapis are at risk because they live in only one place in the world. If okapis lose this **habitat**, they will be in danger. A habitat is a place where an animal or plant usually lives. People are cutting down trees in the Ituri Forest to build roads and houses. If the Ituri Forest disappears, okapis will have no place to live.

To stop this, people are working to save okapis and the Ituri Forest. In 1992, the Okapi Wildlife Preserve was created in the Ituri Forest. In this place, people cannot cut down trees or build houses. Hunters cannot kill the okapis that live there. However, wars in the area have made it hard to take care of this preserve. This puts okapis in danger again.

People are also raising okapis in zoos. Today, there are more than 100 okapis in zoos around the world. Scientists study these animals to learn more about them. By doing this, they hope to make sure that there will always be okapis.

Every year people learn more about these special animals. Some scientists even travel to the Ituri Forest to watch wild okapis. There, they teach people the value of saving these animals. There are still many questions scientists want to answer. They want to know how much food okapis need, and how they use the rain forest.

It is hard to count okapis because they hide very well. Today, scientists think there are about 30,000 wild okapis. If people keep the Ituri Forest safe, these okapis will continue to survive in their rain forest homes.

long neck
see page 17

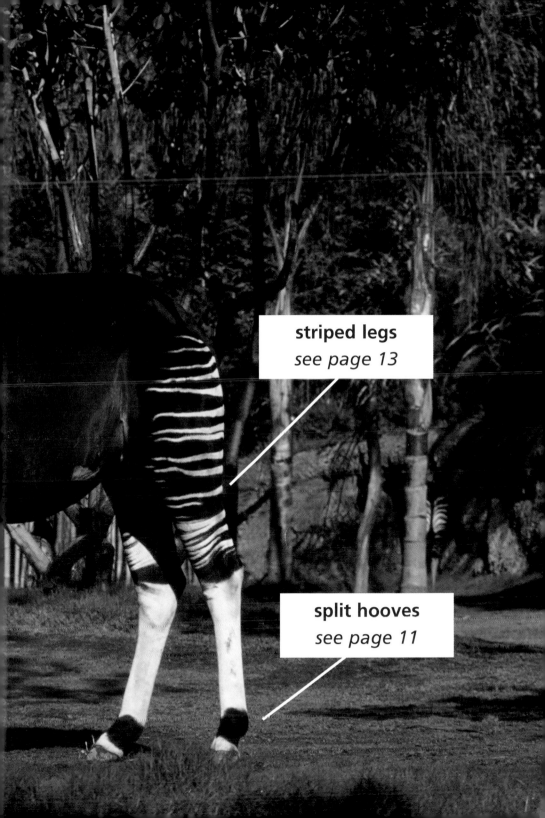

striped legs
see page 13

split hooves
see page 11

Glossary

camouflage—colors, shapes, and patterns that make something blend in with its background

diurnal—active during the day

endangered—an animal that might die out

grooming—the act of cleaning oneself or another's body

habitat—the place where an animal or plant usually lives

herbivores—animals that eat only plants and tree parts

nursing—when a mother feeds her young the milk made inside her body

predator—an animal that hunts other animals for food

prehensile—able to hold or grasp

regurgitate—to bring food back up out of the stomach into the mouth

ruminant—a hoofed animal with a four-chambered stomach that regurgitates its food

Internet Sites

African Forest: Okapi
http://www.colszoo.org/animalareas/aforest/
okapi.html

Endangered Species Report—Okapi
http://www.sandiegozoo.com/special/abcnews/
abcnews_okapi.html

Useful Address

Wildlife Conservation Society
2300 Southern Boulevard
Bronx, NY 10460

Books to Read

Green, Mary Neel. *What Am I?* Austin, TX:
University of Texas Press, 1999.

Moser, Madeline. *Ever Heard of an Aardwolf?*: A
Miscellany of Uncommon Animals. San Diego:
Harcourt Brace & Co., 1996.

Index